The Absolute Quickest W. a Window Cleaning Business!

How to start a successful Window

Cleaning Business Fast and Easy!

Bernard Savage

Contents:

Chapter 1

How to easily start a window cleaning business!

Start your own window cleaning business or a window washing business by using our information gathered from over 35 years being in the detailing industry.

If you have been thinking about starting a window cleaning business, this book will give you all the information for washing, and window cleaning start up tips!

Did you know professional's window cleaner can easily earn in excess of $350.00 a day?

Starting a window cleaning business of your own is one of the easiest of all small businesses to start. And the window cleaning business industry is a "billion dollar business"! The initial start-up costs are well within your reach, and the margin of profit ratio very high!

Window cleaning business is an easy business to operate, and yet one that will always be necessary, as long as people live in houses. It has a very high rating on all business stability charts, and once started; your window cleaning business will grow quickly and begin making a considerable amount of money.

When you own your window cleaning business,

there will be no more punching a time clock, working somewhere or for someone you really don't like, and working hard for someone else just so they can earn all of the money. And best of all, the personal satisfaction you will gain from being successful and turning nothing into something. All it takes to be successful in any business is the will and determination.

First of all, you will need to decide exactly what you want the business to be. You can either have a small one man window cleaning business, or grow it into one with multiple employees and mobile window cleaning vans, or even, someday become the biggest window cleaning business nationwide! There is no limit to what you can do!

You will need to decide if you want to start it full time or begin slowly by working part time. If you have the funds to go out and buy all the equipment for a start-up window cleaning business, or to start small and slowly build up the funds to buy more and bigger and better equipment, do what fits your situation.

Before starting a window cleaning business, gain experience in window cleaning by working as an employee or apprentice for a window cleaning company. This experience provides you with customer service skills, the knowledge of how to wash different types of windows, and how to run your own business. A successful window cleaning business should provide quality care and offer services, such as wash screen doors, and cleaning gutters.

Create a business plan to help you stay focused during each stage of business development. Divide your plan into four or five sections. Include information about the types of window cleaning services you plan to provide in the first section. Focus on residential, or one level building, depending on your interest and skills. Additional services include high rise office building, high rise condos, and high rise apartment. Provide a list of window cleaning equipment and supplies needed to run your business in the second section and include the cost of these items. Outline day-to-day expenses, such as phone, Internet, transportation, and employee costs in the third section. Describe how you plan to market your window washing business in the fourth section. Estimate how much you plan to earn in your first year of business in the fifth section.

You should choose a location for your business. If you plan to work from home, create a space for an office to receive calls, store equipment, complete bookkeeping duties, and store files. Contact local commercial real estate agents to inquire about leasing a space for your business.

Purchase business insurance such as general liability, workers' compensation if hiring employees, product insurance, or home-based business insurance to protect business assets in the event of a lawsuit or settlement. Worker's compensation insurance covers employee accident or injury when on the job. You may also need to purchase a surety bond. A surety bond helps promote an honest relationship between business owner and customer. In the event of a lawsuit or settlement, the state of Kentucky may use the bond to pay for legal expenses.

Apply for a business license by contacting the Fayette County Clerk's Office, if opening a window cleaning business in Lexington, or the county clerk's office that serves the county where you want to conduct business. Contact the Kentucky Secretary of State Office to register your business, if forming a corporation, limited liability company, or partnership.

Chapter 2

Simple way to get a Business License:

If you're trying starting a home based window cleaning business, in most counties you must have a business license. It is the law. If you try to run a business without a business license, you will be fined or, in some counties, arrested.

Do you need insurance to get a window cleaning license? If you're operating a window cleaning business in Fayette County, Kentucky, you don't need insurance to get a license. Different states and counties have their own laws when it comes in regard to license and insurance. In order to find out what's needed in your county, call the County

Clerk's office. They will tell you what you'll need to do.

First, decide what you want to name your business. Look for something snappy and easy to remember. I have put together a few names to give you an idea. You are welcome to use any name but be sure no one else is using the names in your state. Check with the County Clerk's office.

*Clear View

*Snappy Window Cleaning

*Bright Window Cleaning

*Clean Windows How

*Spotless Window Cleaners

*Squeaky Clean Windows

* Perfect Vision Window Cleaning

*Clear View Window Cleaning Service

Some home businesses believe if their company has a professional name, it will help them get more clients. I disagree. It doesn't matter what you call your business. If you follow the plan in this book, your business will be successful.

This is what I did. I wrote down several names for my window cleaning business. Next, I talked to several friends, asking them what service sounds more professional and which name caught their attention.

That's what you're looking for a name that captures the client's attention.

Once you come up with the name, call your local Commissioner of Revenue Office, which is located in the County Clerk's office in the county governments building. They will help you get a business license. They'll need to know what business you will be running and your business address. You must live in the county where your window cleaning business is located.

If you go to another county and pick-up

customers, you may have to pay a county tax for that area. Once again, contract the County Clerk's office to find out the laws.

This is how it works. If you live in Fayette County but you start pick-up accounts in Franklin County, 12 miles down the road, Franklin's Commissioner of Revenue Office may want their 4.5% annual taxes for you doing business in their County. I know it sucks, but it is the law. I would rather pay $30 to $50 per year in county taxes than to be fined $300 to $500 for not paying taxes.

Some Counties may check the Zoning Department to make sure your residence is zoned for a window cleaning business. I have never heard of a county refusing to give license to a window cleaning business unless you have a fleet of vehicles and a 30 mean operation. If that was the case, you wouldn't need this book, you would be writing one.

Will you need a Tax ID Number? I don't think so. If a man is going to hire you to wash his windows, I don't think he'll be worry about a Tax ID Number. He'll want his window cleaning.

Do you have employees or plan on hiring someone in the next few weeks? I wouldn't think about hire anyone until I have more business the I can handle. Once that happens, I will hire someone part-time. When you're hiring full-time employees, it's time to get your Tax Id Number, Social Security, and Worker's Compensation insurance.

Do I need Worker's Compensation Insurance? If you hiring employees, yes. If your employee falls through a window getting injured, you will need insurance for protection.

"Google" Worker's Compensation Insurance. It will direct you to several sites where you can find a list of agents in your area.

Do you need liability insurance to start a window cleaning business? In the state of Kentucky, you do not need liability insurance to get license. But I would check my Commissioner of Revenue Office to be on the safe side. If they do request liability insurance, I would work alone until I have the money to get the correct insurance.

This is my opinion. If an employee get injured falling through a window, I don't have $2000 to $5000 to pay an employee's doctor bill. It will shut my business down before I get the doors open. Get the insurance and keep it as long as you're in business.

The reason for liability insurance is to protect your business just in case something, like an employee getting injured, happens. But that's my opinion. It's it left up to you.

Chapter 3

The best way to start your business!

Now you have your business license and insurance, next is the location.

Most small window cleaning businesses do not have an office because they go to their customer's homes to wash windows. The only thing you'll need is a phone to take calls, and window cleaning equipment and supplies.

If you have a lot of supplies, you will need a spare room. Or, basement would be perfect. Some place you can clean out put down an in-door; -out-door carpet. This room or rooms should be clean and smoke free.

It's my opinion that if you are a smoker, doesn't smoke in a confined room with the equipment. Wait until you leave the room. I'm not trying to rag on you if you're a smoker, that's your business. But there are people who don't want their home smelling like cigarette smoke. But if you are a smoker, make sure the area where you keep the supplies and tools is smoke free.

Keep a report on every window you clean. This will tell you the date of service, what the customer wanted, condition of the windows, what you did, and how much it cost. The customers know their windows. They are the boss. Do what they tell you, when they tell you, and you will have a happy client. If a customer requests washing windows with no window cleaner don't try to talk them into a gutter cleaning detailing just to run up their bill. Wash the windows, have the customer signs your receipt, and move on to the next job. Be honest, giving them what they pay for and thanking them for the business, and move on the next job.

You are professional. Make daily notes on every job. This is very important which is why I'm saying it again. If you purchase a special window cleaner because your client requested it, get two receipts one for you and the one the customer.

If you see any gouges, spatter marks, cracks and indentations on the windows, call the owner right away. Take pictures, record the time, date, and anything the owner says, and keep it in your files. If you have a witness, gets a statement from them about what they saw.

Get the statement in writing and put it in your files. When the owner pays you for your work, have them sign a statement about what you reported and what they said and give them a copy.

Do not tell the owner about your picture or about the witness's statement. Protect yourself and your business.

Keep your equipment area clean. Your vehicle and the window cleaning equipment are the first things the clients see. It should be cleaned every night when you return home and detailed once a week.

When you complete the service, make sure you thank them for their service. Let them know how much you enjoyed cleaning their windows. Three days later, mail them a thank you letter, letting them know again how much you enjoyed cleaning their windows and look forward to doing it again. This simple letter will help your future relationship with the client.

People wonder how we are able to keep clients

coming back year after, year, after, year. I'm going to tell you the secret of keeping your clients coming back. On every holiday, mail them a card thanking them for their business. On Christmas, we send our clients a box of Christmas cookies and a Christmas card. On Mother's Day, Father's Day, Easter, and the 4th of July, we never forget our clients. If we do this, 90% of our clients always come back.

Sounds simple, doesn't it? Well, try it, my friend. It's worked for me and it will work for you.

One of the most important things to remember when the customers start using your service is to ask them how they heard about you. This simple marketing tool will help you use your advertising dollars more wisely.

You should also ask them, "Who wash your windows before and why is they still them no longer washing your windows?" Use any valuable information gathered as a ways of promoting your business.

Chapter 4

Quickest, Cheapest way to Getting Customers!

Like gas to a fire, clients are the life force to any business. Customers pay your bills, put gas in your car, feed you, and keep your business operating in a professional way. Just like any business, you need customers to stay in business. Not one or two but a steady stream of clients.

Let me tell you how I got my first 10 clients with 25 flyers. In a residential area where 1500 square foot three bedroom homes. I walked the area, talking to the people and, handing out flyers. I notice that 35% were the working families, and others, retired people, that didn't have the time to wash their windows the way it should be done.

I would introduce myself, asking them, "Who washes your windows?" Once we started talking, and I'm getting feedback, I would offer to wash two windows free.

If the customer was using another window cleaning service, I would ask them the following questions;

What are you looking for in a window cleaning service?

Who clean your window?

Are you happy with the service?

How did you find out about the service?

What could this service do better?

How much do they charge?

Do not put down or talk about another window cleaning business. This is unprofessional. It is wrong and bad business. If the customers have something bad to say about another, listen and take note but do not voice an opinion. If you don't have something nice to say about another man's business, don't say anything.

Keep notes on the customer's replies and use

this information to market and improve your window cleaning business. Always ask them how they heard about the window cleaning service. This simple marketing tool will help you advert more wisely.

This is valuable information if you are new to the business. It lets you know what has made the other business successful and what works in that area.

A good marketing system is using what other people say to market your business. If I talk with 18 clients who say, "We love Kelly's Window Cleaning Service because he uses that new window washing solution by Windex," when I talk with my next customers, I say; "At Spotless Window Cleaning, we use Windex window cleaning, produces." You can learn a lot from talking with people, and you may also pick- up new customers.

That's why we ask the clients about their window cleaning. If a client is looking for another window cleaner, I ask them. "Weren't you happy with the service of Kelly's Window Cleaning? I heard they have a good system."

"No, he smoked while cleaning my windows and my windows smelled like cigarettes. It took me a month to get the smell out of my house."

"Pete, at Spotless Window, we have a smoke free team who will take care of your window cleaning needs."

Talk to your customers, learn what they like and dislike about the other window cleaning services, and then think how you can better your service.

Pricing your service is also very simple, if you know what to do. Talk to your customers to find out how much the other services are charging. You can also call or walk-in their place of business and ask. We don't believe in low bidding just to get clients. But we believe in a fare bid. If the going rate is $8 to $15 a window, I would charge $12 per window for my service.

We offer clean two windows free to anyone who signs up for bi-monthly window cleaning service. Free is one of the strongest words in the business industry. By offering something or anything free, you will opens the door just wide enough to get your feet in. Even in the hardest markets.

Take before and after pictures of a few homes. If you are new to the business, this gives you visual proof of your skills in window cleaning. It also provides you with the opportunity to master your craft. Remember what they say! Practices makes perfect.

If you don't have any money to start your

window cleaning business, there's other ways that you can get clients within the next 7 days, using the people you know. This way is simple but very successful and people are using it every day.

Sit down and make a list of everyone you know. Make list family members, friends, and neighbors, and their landlords or property managers and acquaintances. You need their addresses and phone numbers.

Start with your family and friends. You can call them, but I think it's better to talk with them face-to-face. Let everyone know you are starting a window cleaning business and ask for help.

What you are trying to do is get a list of people who would like window cleaning services. Everyone needs their window cleaning; people just don't have the time, so it's better to hire someone you know than to bring a stranger to your home.

Talk with your spouse; and make a list of all the people she knows. People she works with, church members, gym members, and acquaintances.

Acquaintances are people like your doctor, dentist, mailman, landlord, and veterinarian. Talk with your children and get the names of their teachers, their best friend's parents, and school bus driver.

You can keep your list growing by asking family,

friends, neighbors, and acquaintances to fill-out a list of everyone they know. Let people know that this information is very important and you'll need it as soon as possible.

What I did is call everyone on my list and invited them to a chili dinner. Who doesn't love chili? It's cheap to make and most people will not turn down a free meal. Over 22 people showed up, and I told them about my window cleaning business and, asking them to write down everyone who lived in a house before leaving my home. To my amazement, I picked up 5 customers and a list of 35 possible customers.

I also made a special offer to the people I invited

to the chili dinner. If anyone on their list used my service, we would give them $20.00.

One guy called his uncle, who owned two strip malls and was looking for a professional window washer. The next day, I sat down with the guy and we came up with a fair agreement and his nephew received $100.00.

Let's look at it this way. My investment was $35.00 for the business license, and $60.00 for the chili. This one account turns out to be a $10,000 per year account. Not bad, not bad at all.

For the next 2 weeks, I worked the list, mailing out letters and phone calls, pulling in 12 more clients.

17 customers

Estimate 1st 3 Weeks Income $650

Every client is a walking advertisement. Your clients can get you customers quicker than any T.V. or Radio advertisement. Once I had established myself, I made the following offer to my clients, 25% off for every new customer referred to me. Free window cleaning services for every three customers. That word "Free" worked its magic, pulling in 12 new customers in 2 weeks.

You can use this same offer to turn your window cleaning service into a 6 figure yearly income. It works better for people with a big family or a lot of friends. The more people they know, the longer your mailing list. The longer your mailing list, the more customers you will get.

If you are trying to start the window cleaning business but you have no start-up money and have bad credit, then you must put together a money making plan that will help you to get your business started without investing any money. You can start a window cleaning business without money, but it will require some work and the help of friends and family.

Offer to pay cash for each new customer who is sent to you by friends, neighbors, and family. You should use a cash offer that will not take too much of your profit. A fair amount to offer is $20 per new customer, if profits from the business allow. Explain that as soon as the customer pays you, you will pay for the referral.

Make a flyer on your computer and print out copies to hand out to people in the neighborhood, friends, family members, and anyone you meet who expresses an interest in your business.

I offered $20, to my friends, neighbors, or family for every new customer referred to me. I made the same offer to new customers, $20 or 25% off for every new customer referred to me.

Rent-A-Center made tons on money using this same system on their rentals. Offering their customers half off their next payment, or the next payments free, for every new customer referred to them. Now, banks are using it. My bank pays their customer $50.00 for every new account they referred to them. It is simple. It's a way to get customers without investing any money and it works.

Get Mother to have a Bake Sell:

People love cookies, cakes, pies, and cupcakes, and are willing to pay a little more money for cookies they didn't have to make themselves. Because cupcakes are inexpensive, easy, and quick to make, they are an ideal business start-up project. Get together with your friends, family members, and neighbors to hold a window cleaning business fundraiser. You might be surprised by how much money you can earn for your business start-up capital. I have a friend who started an office cleaning business using this idea three years ago and now am earning over $300,000.00 a year.

You need to set the time and date for your fundraiser. Because cupcakes are good if the weather is cold or hot, they can be held at any time of year, but mother and grandmother needs to know ahead of time to giving them enough time to make their worlds famous chocolate chips cookies.

My mother and girlfriend had spent three days baking cookies for my detailing fundraiser. We went to the Dollar Tree and purchased several boxes of freezer bags and I stuffed them with cookies. I talked to the manager of a local Kroger and asked him about setting up on the sidewalk outside the entrance. He asked what it was for and I said, "A fundraiser." I offered him a dozen of my mother's world-famous chocolate chip cookies and with a smile, he agreed.

Set your prices. The last time we paid for a dozen of cookies from Sam's Club, it cost me $6.50. We a dozen homemade cookies for $10.00 and sold out. We earn over $800.00 dollars in 4 hours. We all agreed with splitting up the money, $150.00 for my mother, $150.00 for my girlfriend, and $500.00 for my window cleaning business. That was how a broke man started his window cleaning service.

Ask current clients if you can post a company sign in their yard as you wash their window, and see if they will allow you to leave it there for a couple days after you complete the job. Offer a promotional discount to those who allow you to advertise your business this way.

If you do a great job with each and every client, they will recommend you to their friends. Make follow-up calls after a job is completed to see that clients are satisfied with your work. Ask them to refer you to friends and family. This is another good way to get started in this business with no money, and free advertisement, is let your work talk for you. Do a thorough job and pay close attention to details. Be meticulous so you do not overlook anything that needs fixing.

Do a walk through with your customer. The most important parts of this business are to make sure your customer is pleased with your service.

How about a local fish fry? If you like to fish or

have a friend who's a fisherman, people love fried fish. You could charge up to $7.00 for a fish sandwich and $10.00 for a plate. You can get some baked beans and coleslaw for the plate or meal.

I had a cousin who opened a Lawn Care Service. He didn't have any money, car, lawn mower, trimmer, or blower. After selling fish every Friday and Saturday for 2 months, he was able to get all the equipment needed to start his business.

Chili worked for me. On a cool fall weekend, Saturday and Sunday after church, there's nothing better than a hot bowl of chili or soup.

The best way to advertise your chili, fish fry, or any food sale is churches and word of mouth. Make some flyers with "Fish Fry" or "Hot Chili" at the top, with your name, phone number, times, and dates on the bottom. Passing out the flyers in your neighborhood or placing those on cars at local churches should get a lot of business. If you ask a week or two before the before the date of the sale, some churches may announce your sale to their members. This will work better if you offer to donate 10 to 15% of the profits to the church.

Make a list of everyone you know, and tell them about your food sale. Don't forget to tell them you're trying to earn money to start-up a window cleaning business. Most true friends will want to help you so the more people who knows what you are trying to do, the better for your business. Ask them to call and tell everyone they know and ask them to do the same.

HOT CHILI

SALE

FOR WINDOW WASHING BUSINESS

START-UP CAPITAL

PLEASE HELP!

438 RACE STREET

1 PM- TO- 7PM

FIRDAY, SATURDAY, & SUNDAY

DATE:

Vegetable Soup

Chicken Noodle

Soup

(Sale)

FOR WINDOW WASHING BUSINESS

START-UP CAPITAL

PLEASE HELP!

438 RACE STREET

1 PM- TO- 7PM

FIRDAY, SATURDAY, & SUNDAY

DATE:

FRIED FISH

SALE

FOR WINDOW WASHING BUSINESS

START-UP CAPITAL

PLEASE HELP!

438 RACE STREET

1 PM- TO- 7PM

FIRDAY, SATURDAY, & SUNDAY

DATE:

SWEET BAKE GOODS

SALE

FOR CAR WINDOW CLEANING BUSINESS

START-UP CAPITAL

PLEASE HELP!

438 RACE STREET

1 PM- TO- 7PM

FIRDAY, SATURDAY, & SUNDAY

DATE:

Chapter 5

How to find the best customers fast!

We offer on-site window washing for residents, and commercial properties.

Our clients list:

Residents	Grocery Store
Auto Dealerships	Convenience Store
Churches	Liquor Store
Daycare Centers	Restaurants
Banks	Office Business
Doctor Offices	Drug Stores
Service Station	Fitness Gyms

Build Your Window Cleaning Business

Fast with Flyers!

Homemade flyers are a great way to promote both large and small window cleaning services. It's possible to design a flyer on your home computer or by having one created for a small fee by a local printing company. Regardless of how the flyer is made, they all serve the same purpose, which is marketing, for your window cleaning business.

Local businesses, such as the local grocery store or hardware shop, will generally have a board for local advertising. Any business is free to hang their flyer or business card on these designated areas.

Passing them out in a neighborhood is a great way to get flyers into a customer's hands. First, check with their local laws as some areas do not allow this form of marketing. However, for those that do, handing out flyers at places such as the fair in town, the food court in the mall, or at a flea market are just a few suggestions where how one might use a flyer.

You need to pass out flyers to everyone you think might be interested. Be sure you approach pedestrians in a public area and that you don't block anyone's way. Don't be afraid to approach people, as they're probably shyer about getting the flyer than you are about handing it out. Answer any questions about the information presented on your flyer. Be friendly and smile because you could be talking to a future customer.

I would not leave flyers off on doorsteps because someone may slip on it and fall. Put in mail slots if your flyer is applicable to the area. This is a good approach for advertising your window cleaning business.

Keep up your distribution efforts for as long as possible. You might reach someone you didn't the first time. If your flyer is torn down or removed, put a new one up. I found out years ago that persistence pays off.

Years ago, after I was discharged from the service, I read a book called, How to Start a Delivery Service. It was a little 50 page paperback loaded with tons of information. On the section about promoting your business, it had information that I still use today. He called it flooding your market and this is how it works.

This is a trick to pulling in customers in the same area, cutting your cost in gas from this area to another. Plus, when a customer sees your business name in their faces three or four times a month, when it is time to wash windows, they think about you.

This little secret technique has always worked over the years. I call it working an area. If you are dropping off flyers door-to-door or mailing your flyers to a mailing list, work your list until your clients call you and tell you to stop dropping off your flyers.

You see proof that this system works every week. Think about it. How many times do you get fast food, automobile oil change, and department store coupons every month? Even if you never go to that store, restaurant, or oil change service, once or twice a month, every month, you receive the same ads from the same companies. These companies are spending thousands of dollars every month, month after month, year after year.

Why? Because it works, and it will work for you, believe me. I tested it and it will make you money.

Dropping your business flyers at a front door or tucked in a screen is legal unless the homeowner or resident has posted a "no solicitation" or "no distribution" sign. If a property owner/resident has ordered a flyer distributor off his property and the person comes back, the police may be called, and fines, trespassing charges, or other criminal charges may result. But if you see any flyers or door hangers on the door, it is safe.

The easy way to make effective flyers:

What kind of paper should you use? When picking the paper for your flyers, which you can find at any copy shop, such as Quick Print, Copy Express, or Office Max, decide on a color, preferably something that will stand out so people will remember the flyer.

Start off with something at the top of your flyer that will capture your customer's attention. How about "First Window Cleaning 50% off For the First 20 Customers Who Calls." You can have the coupon at the top to grab people's interest. Add an incentive for keeping the flyer, such as a, "$50.00 Complete Window Cleaning for the First 30 People Who Calls." If you are making this offer, your phone will be ringing off the hook. I have had customers calling me at 5 o'clock in the morning, wanting to know if the offer is still good.

This is how it works. When the customer calls you, respond to the call as soon as possible. Be on time; and do your best job and when you've completed cleaning their windows, gives them your business card.

You know what services they want and how long it takes to clean their windows. What I say to them is, "Thank you for using our service. When would you like your next window service?" You will be amazed by how well this works.

According to the Direct Marketing Association, flyers and door hanger's response rates are usually between 1 and 3 percent.

That means you should get one or three phone calls out of every 100 flyers you put out, if your flyer looks good and catch your customer's attention. But by adding, (Call today and get 50% off your window cleaning) on my flyers', my response jumped to 6 to 8 percent. Call for 50% off on your first Window

Cleaning, or (Call today and we will wash your windows for only $40.00). Six customers responded, and out of the six, four called back for the complete service two months later.

But in order to get my phone ringing faster, I added this: (This offer is only available to the first 20 Customers, please be the first to call "(your number"). This works, trust me. You will get so many clients; you will not know what to do with them. This simple little technique will give you all the business you need.

What do I do when the phone starts ringing? I give this offer to everyone and. I do not care if they are number 25. If it is possible for us to clean their windows in the next few days, I am there, doing my best to make that client happy.

I know what you're thinking; if I make this offer, I am going to get ripped off. The truth is that most people will not rip you off. Yes, some may not become regular clients, but more will. The best part about this offer is most detailing services will not make this offer; which will open the door for you.

Save Money By Using Door Hangers:

What are door hangers? They are rectangular in shape and are longer than they are wide. They have a circular hole near the top to slide them onto a doorknob. Each door hanger contains a message for the customer, with information about your window cleaning service. This message can be a special offer for services in their neighborhood. Sometimes, door hangers are used for decoration.

I use more door hangers the flyers to advertise my window cleaning business. Have door hangers made with your business logo, company name, and contact information. Hand them out or pay to have various hotels or restaurants give them out to their customers.

Put out 600 door hangers in a chosen area once a week for the next ten weeks. Ten weeks putting out-door hangers- on the same doors, over and over again.

Your response rate will be amazing, cutting your gas rate down, and raising your profits ratio, putting more money in your pockets.

My door hangers had a big title that said, "Call us today and we will wash your windows for only $35.00, if you are the first of 20 customers to call (No Obligations)" along with an eye-catching and dramatic color photo. We found this little wording on door hangers caused folks to at least check the body of the message.

How to Make Door Hanger At Home:

By using your computer or a friend's computer, you can make your own door hangers from home. This is what I do.

Go into All Programs and select a word processing program such as Microsoft Office, Microsoft Word, or Open Office Writer. Click on the "format" tab and select "columns". Choose a minimum of three columns and click "ok".

Change your page layout to land-scape by clicking on the "file" and selecting "page set-up". Choose "land-scape" and click "ok".

Next, you can begin designing your door hanger flyers. You will be able to fit three on a page, one per column. Make sure to include your contact information and the name of your product and service, and your attention catching offers. Attention grabbing offer goes across the top of the page in bold print. This should be the first thing your customers see.

Next, you should print out your first draft and ask some family members or neighbors for their opinions. Have them check for spelling errors, typos, and errors in consistency. Have them make suggestions on how to improve your flyer. Make any suggested changes and have your proofreaders check the flyer one last time.

If you decide to use black and white photos or no photos at all, and then it is fine to print your flyers in black and white.

The first printing of new detailing service flyers should be small, 300 or 500 are enough. Hand these out and measure your response rate by keeping track of who calls. You may decide to do this with a special offer that you have only advertised on your flyers. Like; (: Call us today and we will wash your windows for $35.00.)

We put out a ton of flyers and door hangers each week. The best way to do it is to hire a couple kids and pay them by the flyer. Paying them 4 cents per flyer and it makes them work faster.

You can also contact the area newspaper distributor and ask him to include your flyer in his distribution along with newspaper. They have fixed rates generally.

Flyer Delivery Service,

These companies are professional and looking for long-term customers. I look for the service that has that has been in business for ten years or longer. I also ask for reference. They will professionally design your flyers and deliver them for a fee.

Chapter 6

How to keep customers happy:

You've written a sales letter that you think is going to knock their socks off. (See if you haven't yet.) Before mailing it out, have a look at these sales letters tips to make ensure you're maximizing the return on your sales letter campaign.

Mail Your Sales Letter To The Right People:

If the intent of your sales letter is to advertise window cleaning services. Even though the best mailing list is one that you've built personally from your own prospect list, we use the yellow pages to focus your sales letter campaign on specific categories of potential customers. You can also buy mailing lists from mailing list brokers.

All your customers or clients are not the same. So why should you expect them all to be persuaded by exactly the same sales letter? Create different versions of your sales letter for different segments of your target market by emphasizing different benefits of your offer or by changing the benefits completely.

Writing the name and address of the recipient directly onto the envelope will increase your sales letter response. Also, direct marketing studies have shown that having names and addresses handwritten is the surest way to get your sales letter opened. However, this may not be appropriate for your business image.

Get a ton of business by re-mailing 2 or 3 weeks later.

If you've forgotten everything else in this book, remember this: sending out another mailing to the same list should get a response of about half the original response. Not bad at all when the work is already done!

Besides sending your sales letter to prospective customers through the mail, you might also use email. However, be aware that people generally are more receptive to unsolicited mail arriving through the mail than to unsolicited email.

In the next few pages, you will find some of the most successful sales letters we used to turn our business from a small, two man operations to over $150,000.00 a year, window cleaning business.

We began with door hanger and weeks later, decided onto mailing them out.

First, we put together a mailing list. We used the local yellow pages to get the names and addresses of, auto dealerships, grocery stores, daycare centers, and restaurants, in every town within 50 miles of our business.

Re-mailing is the secret to success in this business. Once we had our mailing list of over 400 companies, we mailed out the first sales letter to the first 100 customers on a Sunday night. A week later, we mail out the same letter to the next 100. We did this once a week for a month.

We followed up with the second sales letter the following month and the next letter the following month.

What was our response ratio? Let me put it this way. Within three months, we had 2 car dealerships, 2 grocery stores, 5 daycare centers and 4 churches, which is enough work to keep 4 full-time employees busy five days a week.

Best prices to charge for your service;

My rates are based on rates in my area in Central Kentucky. We came up with these prices after talking with customers and other window washing businesses. Before you price your services, talk to window washing businesses and customers in your area.

We charge $8.00 per window for residents, and $10.00 to $15.00 for commercial properties. If you bid around those rates we will win 90% of your bids.

On the next pages, you will find some flyers used by other successful pet grooming services. You are welcome to try them or make up your own. They have worked for me, so maybe they'll work for you.

Spotless Window Cleaning Service

Phone

If you're like most of our customers, you have a to-do list a mile long. Between taking the kids to soccer, shopping for groceries, or a big project at work, life keeps you busy. Let our professional take window cleaning off your list. Whether you're tackling spring cleaning or preparing for the holidays, we can remove one of your headaches.

Be the next to call and get 50% off your window cleaning!

You'll have peace of mind

knowing training professionals

are cleaning your windows!

Spotless Window Cleaning Service

Phone

Clean windows can change your worldview, literally! Your windows, covered in fingerprints and residue will be transformed by our expertise. Once you see how clean and clear your windows can look you will never want to see them any other way! Regular cleaning and care of your windows can prolong their life-time.

Be the next to call and get 50% off your window cleaning!

You'll have peace of mind

knowing training professionals

are cleaning your windows!

Spotless Window Cleaning Service

Phone

There is nothing more cost effective to improve the appearance and showcase your home than to have your windows professionally cleaned. We exclusively clean residential properties 1 and 2 story structures.

Be the next to call and get 50% off your window cleaning!

You'll have peace of mind

knowing training professionals

are cleaning your windows!

Spotless Window Cleaning Service

Phone

Give a professional first impression of your company with crystal-clear windows. We offers commercial window cleaning services to businesses. We clean windows on one stories building as well.

Be the next to call and get 50% off your window cleaning!

You'll have peace of mind

knowing training professionals

are cleaning your windows!

Spotless Window Cleaning Service

Phone

Many of our Customers are Residential Ones, just like YOU! We pride ourselves on offering very reliable service at competitive prices. We've been around the local area for over 10 years. Many of our Customers have been with us from the beginning. Others we have come to know year after year. Throughout the years we have consistently maintained our service and integrity while delivering exceptional quality.

Be the next to call and get 50% off your window cleaning!

You'll have peace of mind

knowing training professionals

are cleaning your windows!

Spotless Window Cleaning Service

Phone

Although the majority of our business is in the Residential, we have many regular business which rely on our services. Just as with all our customers we will deliver to you the same prompt and reliable service that is our trademark of excellence. Call us for quote we will get back to in a timely fashion.

Be the next to call and get 50% off your window cleaning!

You'll have peace of mind

knowing training professionals

are cleaning your windows!

Spotless Window Cleaning Service

Phone

We cleaned a lot of windows in the past 10 years, and if there's one thing we've learned, it's this: Sparkling windows are not only a reflection on your business; they're a reflection on ours. That's why we guarantee your satisfaction with every job. Our exceptional quality and service are unmatched.

Be the next to call and get 50% off your window cleaning!

You'll have peace of mind

knowing training professionals

are cleaning your windows!

Spotless Window Cleaning Service

Phone

The right tool for the right job is the key to perfectly clean windows. Our specially formulated window cleaner allow the window to stay wet longer and the squeegee slide easily across the window.

Be the next to call and get 50% off your window cleaning!

You'll have peace of mind

knowing training professionals

are cleaning your windows!

Spotless Window Cleaning Service

Phone

The very first time you employ our Window Washing Team, it is strongly recommended that you have your windows cleaned both inside and out including screens too. Why have clean windows and look through dirty screens. However, if you prefer, we will do just the outside with or without the screens. We try to accommodate each and every single person with the ultimate goal of gaining another satisfied customer.

Be the next to call and get 50% off your window cleaning!

You'll have peace of mind

knowing training professionals

are cleaning your windows!

Spotless Window Cleaning Service

Phone

Regular cleaning of windows is an essential part of home or building maintenance. We recommend that windows be cleaned four times per year to avoid damaging and stubborn buildup of stains. We provides a streak-free clean every time, providing clarity and a brighter out-look.

Be the next to call and get 50% off your window cleaning!

You'll have peace of mind

knowing training professionals

are cleaning your windows!

Spotless Window Cleaning Service

Phone

We has been cleaning residential and commercial windows for more than 10 years. Our crews are experienced enough to deal with any difficult situation and responsible enough to do it in a quick and professional manner.

Be the next to call and get 50% off your window cleaning!

You'll have peace of mind

knowing training professionals

are cleaning your windows!

Spotless Window Cleaning Service

Phone

Window cleaning is a difficult task. Dirt, grime, mineral deposits and the harsh weather can make it near impossible to get them perfectly clean. Add to that dangerous ladder work, and the job seems almost impossible. Call us window cleaning is what we do, and we love it!

Be the next to call and get 50% off your window cleaning!

You'll have peace of mind

knowing training professionals

are cleaning your windows!

Spotless Window Cleaning Service

Phone

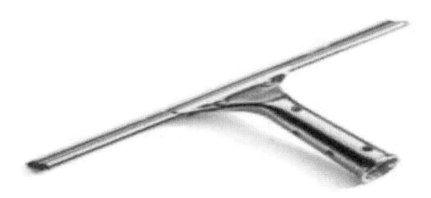

We are reliable window cleaners who pride ourselves on being one of the best, when we quote you for cleaning your windows it includes the cleaning of windows, frames and the sills.

Be the next to call and get 50% off your window cleaning!

You'll have peace of mind

knowing training professionals

are cleaning your windows!

Spotless Window Cleaning Service

Phone

We offers excellent local window washing services with prompt, dependable service at reasonable prices. We provide residential window cleaning services as well as Commercial window cleaning services. We are very flexible and accommodating with our scheduling.

Be the next to call and get 50% off your window cleaning!

You'll have peace of mind

knowing training professionals

are cleaning your windows!

Spotless Window Cleaning Service

Phone

There's nothing like having your windows cleaned and letting the natural light cheer up your home. With thorough attention given to not only your storms, screens, sills, and most importantly your windows we leave your home with a whole outlook...light and fresh.

Be the next to call and get 50% off your window cleaning!

You'll have peace of mind

knowing training professionals

are cleaning your windows!

Spotless Window Cleaning Service

Phone

Don't relish the idea of getting the ladder out, climbing up and clearing your windows? Then you really should to leave the job to the professionals !

Be the next to call and get 50% off your window cleaning!

You'll have peace of mind

knowing training professionals

are cleaning your windows!

Chapter 7

The best way to manage your income!

Warning, warning, warning do! Do try to get too big to fast. This is very, very important. I made that mistake once in this business, using the multi-mailing, and new accounts ringing the phone off the hook. The only thing I saw was dollars. I was too much into making money and was not thinking about running my business. I ended in trouble with the IRS and almost lost everything.

This is a business. When money coming in hand over fist we make the mistake of thinking "I am going enjoy myself, going out purchasing a new customize window washing van and hiring 10 employees." And the next thing you know, reality hits and you are in trouble.

My simple bookkeeping system which has worked for

me for years, is called the 1/4 payroll system. This way everyone is paid. This is how it works. My base rate for window cleaning service is $60.00 per hour. For every hour I work, I pay myself $15.00. I pay my company $15.00 and I pay my employees $15.00 and $15.00 goes in an emergency account.

But the trick to making this work for your business is to leave the money in its account. The purpose for paying yourself is living, buying your food, paying your bills and surviving. The money you pay into your business is for equipment, advertising, and gas. This money keeps your business going year after year. The money for employees can be used in two different ways. If you have an employee, it his pay. If not you build up that account for when you do hire someone.

On the business income, use it for mainly advertising in your first year. I would not buy any new equipment because you are trying to build your business account up for the following season. If you do not have start-up equipment and tools and cannot borrow them, I would check yard sales and flea markets. Someone always has tools for sell. Remember, we are trying to build a business, not to go down the first year.

On employee income, I would not hire any employees unless I reach a point where it is impossible for me to handle the work, and I would hire only part-time employees.

If you make it through the first year and do not have to hire any employees, that is great. But if you follow the steps in this book, one will need help. Every time you groom a pet take out your employee payroll and one must manage one's money carefully.

At the end of the year, the money is counted to make sure it is balanced with the books. If your income taxes are paid quarterly, you take that money out of your business account. If you are paying it yearly, you would send your money in February after your working year, taking the money from your business account. The balance in the business account is put into savings for start-up capital for the following year.

If you have employees, you are stepping on bookkeeper grounds. Finding a good, dependable, low-cost bookkeeper is the way to go. They will handle your employee, business, and personal taxes. If you don't need an employee, save your money for the next year.

Almost 98% of the businesses that go under are run by people who do not plan ahead. They will work hard earning $300 and go out and blow the money in a few days. You earned the money, I cannot tell you what to do with it. But if you want to stay in the window washing business and earn a good income, follow my system.

Good luck my friend.

Printed in Great Britain
by Amazon.co.uk, Ltd.,
Marston Gate.